Let's S1

Kids' Cookbook & Earth Friendly Fun

by Dianne Pratt
illustrated by Janet Winter

Acknowledgements:
Recipes and nutritional information: Thank you Sarah Lanford, Norberta Butler, Robin Pratt, Christine Bird, Carol and Jessica Boudreau, G. William Eldridge
Art ideas: Thank you Janet Winter, Robin and Bobby Pratt
Technical support: Thank you Sherri Eldridge

Credits:
Cover Design, Layout and Typesetting: Dianne Pratt and Sherri Eldridge
Cover and Text Art: Janet Winter
Editing: Sherri Eldridge
Proofreading: G. William Eldridge, Jerry and Fran Goldberg, and Barbara Mills
Research and Development Assistance: Robin and Bobby Pratt

Let's Stir It Up!
Kids' Cookbook & Earth Friendly Fun
by Dianne Pratt

Published by:
Harvest Hill Press
P.O. Box 55, Salisbury Cove, Maine 04672
207-288-8900

ISBN: 1-886862-29-X

First printing: September 1998

Printed in the U.S.A.

10%
__Total Recovered Fiber__
All Post-Consumer Recycled

This book is dedicated to my favorite daddy,
Jim Bird,
whose unwavering love and support have given me
courage and confidence throughout my life.

Introduction

All through the ages, kids just like you have demonstrated a unique curiosity and appreciation for the world around them. With never ending questions and the expression of wonder, you have the ability to inspire adults to take a fresh look at the world.

Throughout this book are recipes, experiments and observation activities, along with ecology, earth, food and animal facts to encourage your curiosity and enthusiasm.

Before beginning any recipe or activity, carefully read through the instructions and collect all the necessary items. Everything needed for your observations and experiments can probably be found in your home and backyard. When you are finished, put everything away and wash any dishes or utensils you've used. Please leave nature and the kitchen the way you found them!

You will also discover how easy it is to make a difference in protecting your planet. It's a good idea to start a notebook in which to record your findings (see pg.31). Be sure to include the date of nature observations and do them again each season of the year. Things can change a lot from one season to the next.

Remember to be safe! Always ask for adult assistance when using tools, knives and appliances, especially the stove and oven.

Okay, you're off and running. Now have fun and...LET'S STIR IT UP!

CONTENTS

Banana Pancakes

TOOLS:
2 medium mixing bowls
hand mixer or fork
measuring cups and spoons
sifter
non-stick spray cooking oil
frying pan
spatula

INGREDIENTS:
1 very ripe banana
1 egg
½ cup plain yogurt
2 tablespoons canola oil
1 cup flour
1 teaspoon baking powder
¼ teaspoon salt
½ teaspoon ground cinnamon

Optional:
3 tablespoons 2%-lowfat milk

Serving: 2 Pancakes Calories: 237
Protein: 6 gm   Carbohydrates: 32 gm
Fat: 9.5 gm   Calcium: 91 mg

1. In a mixing bowl, mash the banana with a fork. Stir in egg, yogurt and canola oil. To make thinner pancakes, add 3 tablespoons of milk.

2. In a separate bowl, sift together flour, baking powder, salt and cinnamon. Add sifted ingredients to mashed banana mixture. Beat with a fork or hand mixer until smooth.

3. Spray frying pan with non-stick cooking oil. Heat pan over medium heat, just until a few drops of water sprinkled on the pan skitter around.

4. For each pancake, pour ¼-cup of batter into hot pan. Cook until pancakes puff up and little bubbles pop on top. (Don't flatten your pancakes with your spatula! You want them to be light and fluffy.)

5. Flip the pancakes over with the spatula and cook the other side until light brown. (You can peek under it by lifting the edge with your spatula.)

If your pancakes are browned on the outside and gooey on the inside, turn the heat down a little bit.

Apple Pecan Topping

Makes 1 Cup

TOOLS:
paring knife
small saucepan
measuring spoons

INGREDIENTS:
2 medium-sized apples
1 tablespoon butter
2 teaspoons honey
½ teaspoon vanilla
2 tablespoons chopped pecans

1. Peel, core and chop apples into small pieces.

2. In small saucepan over low heat, melt butter with honey, vanilla, pecans and chopped apples.

3. Increase heat to medium and stir constantly. Simmer until apple pieces are hot and tender, about 2 minutes.

Spoon over Banana Pancakes, waffles or vanilla ice cream!

Serving: 1/4 Cup   Calories: 103
Protein: 0 gm   Carbohydrates: 14 gm
Fat: 5.5 gm   Calcium: 7 mg

Pumpkin Crumb Muffins

Makes 12 Muffins

TOOLS:
muffin tins
non-stick spray cooking oil
2 medium mixing bowls
measuring cups and spoons
fork and a large spoon

INGREDIENTS:
2 cups flour
½ cup brown sugar
1 tablespoon baking powder
⅔ cup cooked mashed
   pumpkin, fresh or canned
1 cup 2%-lowfat milk
2 eggs
1 teaspoon vanilla
Optional: ½ cup chocolate chips

TOPPING:
6 tablespoons dry oats
1 tablespoon cocoa powder
1 tablespoon brown sugar
1 tablespoon honey

Serving: 1 Muffin	Calories: 157
Protein: 4 gm	Carbohydrates: 31 gm
Fat: 1.5 gm	Calcium: 86 mg

Preheat oven to 350°. Spray muffin tins with non-stick cooking oil.

1. In a mixing bowl, combine flour, brown sugar and baking powder. In a separate bowl, use a fork to blend pumpkin, milk, eggs and vanilla. Add wet mixture to flour mixture, stirring just until moistened.*

2. In a separate bowl, make topping: stir together the oats, cocoa and brown sugar. Add honey and mix until moist and crumbly.

3. Fill muffin cups ⅓-full with batter. Sprinkle a full teaspoon of topping on each muffin, then lightly press it into batter. Bake 20 minutes.

* Add chocolate chips to batter to make muffins *EXTRA Yummy!*

Moon Over Miami

Serves 1

TOOLS:
butter knife
small juice glass
small cup
small frying pan
non-stick spray cooking oil
spatula

INGREDIENTS:
1 slice whole wheat bread
1 teaspoon butter, softened
   at room temperature
1 egg
a pinch each salt and pepper

Serving: 1 Recipe   Calories: 172
Protein: 9 gm   Carbohydrates: 12 gm
Fat: 10 gm   Calcium: 44 mg

1. Butter both sides of the bread. Place juice glass upside down in the middle of the bread and twist rim into bread to cut out circle. Remove hole.

2. Spray frying pan with non-stick cooking oil, then heat pan on stove over medium burner. Break egg into small cup. Place bread in the middle of hot pan, and pour egg into the hole. Fry until underside is golden brown.

3. Flip with spatula. Put cut-out hole into pan to lightly brown. Cook Moon Over Miami until egg is cooked to your liking. Sprinkle with salt and pepper.

Animal Fact:
Until the 1800's, over 30 million bison roamed the plains of North America from the Mississippi River to the Rocky Mountains. Although their numbers today are still not secure, the bison population is increasing thanks to the efforts of private ranchers and preserves.

Ecology Fact:
Almost three-quarters of the Earth's surface is covered by water, yet many water bodies have been polluted or drained low by human consumption. The Florida Everglades is one area where pollution and draining have endangered many wetland plants and animals. Please help conserve our planet's clean water whenever you shower or brush your teeth.

9

Elephant Tortilla Snack

A nutritious after school treat or for an evening snack! Serves 6

TOOLS:

measuring cups
cookie sheet
spatula
small mixing bowl
spoon

INGREDIENTS:

⅓ cup toasted oats,
    see below
½ cup peanut butter
¼ cup honey
6 6-inch flour tortillas

Serving: 1 Roll-up	Calories: 300
Protein: 9 gm	Carbohydrates: 38 gm
Fat: 13.5 gm	Calcium: 55 mg

1. Combine toasted oats, peanut butter and honey in a small mixing bowl. Mix well.

2. Spread 3-tablespoons mixture on a tortilla. Roll into a log and eat up!

Peanut butter-oatmeal spread is also a great dip for celery, carrot sticks and apple slices.

To toast oats: Preheat oven to 350°. Spread rolled oats on a cookie sheet and bake 10 - 15 minutes, until lightly golden. Cool, then store in a tightly covered container. Toasting extra oats is a good idea - they can be used in recipes to replace breadcrumbs or nuts, thereby reducing calories and fat. For better flavor and texture, use whole rolled oats instead of quick oats.

Dip and Dippers

TOOLS:
measuring cups and spoons
small bowl
fork

INGREDIENTS:
1 cup cottage cheese
½ cup finely grated cheddar
   cheese
1 teaspoon dried dill weed
2 teaspoons Worcestershire
   sauce
pinch of salt

DIPPERS:
About 3 cups assorted raw
veggies of your choice: carrots,
celery, broccoli, cauliflower,
green peppers, snow peas,
cucumber, green beans, etc.

Serving: 1/4 Recipe   Calories: 182
Protein: 12 gm   Carbohydrates: 18 gm
Fat: 7.5 gm   Calcium: 179 mg

1. In the small bowl, mash cottage cheese with grated cheddar cheese.

2. Add remaining ingredients and stir to blend well.

"Dip 2-3-4 and Eat 2-3-4; Dip 2-3-4 and Eat...!"

Ecology Fact:
Grasslands are one of the most widespread vegetation types in the world, covering one-fifth of the Earth's land surface. A wide variety of insects and animals depend on grasslands for their survival. One grassland animal is the African Elephant. As human population increases and poaching persists, the numbers of these majestic animals have significantly decreased. You may live far away from Africa, but everyone can help preserve the safety of the African Elephants by never purchasing items made from their ivory tusks.

My Favorite Fruit Salad

There's magic in this marvelous salad. Whatever you want it to be - that's what it becomes! In the Mood for Melon? Do you just go "Bananas for Blueberries"? Here are a few ideas but remember, anything goes!

Serves 4

TOOLS:

knife and cutting board
can opener
large and small mixing bowls
mixing spoon
measuring cups and spoons

INGREDIENTS:

Select a variety of fresh fruit. Cut into bite-sized pieces to make about 4 cups: Apples, bananas, blackberries, grapes, blueberries, cantalope, pears, honeydew melon, kiwi, mandarin oranges, nectarines, oranges, pineapple, tangerines, plums, strawberries, raspberries, peaches, watermelon, etc.

Select one of these Tasty Toppings:

#1: Mix 1-tablespoon flaked coconut with 1-cup whipped topping. Stir into fruit salad.

#2: Mix 1-cup of any flavor yogurt with 1-tablespoon honey, ¼-teaspoon nutmeg and ⅛-teaspoon cinnamon. Stir into fruit.

#3: Mix ¼-cup defrosted orange juice concentrate, 1-tablespoon brown sugar and ¼-cup apple jelly. Stir into fruit.

Nutritional Analysis with Tasty Topping #2:
Serving: 1 Cup
Calories: 141
Protein: 3 gm
Carbohydrates: 32 gm
Fat: 1 gm
Calcium: 105 mg

Creamy Apple Cole Slaw

Serves 4

TOOLS:
grater
paring knife
large mixing bowl
measuring cups and spoons

INGREDIENTS:
½ small head of cabbage
1 large red apple
1 tablespoon apple juice
    concentrate
1 teaspoon lemon juice
1 tablespoon mayonnaise
1 tablespoon plain yogurt
¼ teaspoon cinnamon

Serving: 3/4 Cup	Calories: 81
Protein: 1 gm	Carbohydrates: 17 gm
Fat: 1.5 gm	Calcium: 38 mg

1. With adult assistance, grate cabbage. Cut apple into quarters, cut out the core. Chop apple into small pieces, leaving the peel on for color and texture.

2. In a mixing bowl, combine remaining ingredients. Add grated cabbage and chopped apple, gently stir until mixed.

Ecology Fact:
There are two types of solar energy, active and passive. Active solar energy systems collect the sun's heat on solar panels to produce electricity. In the wide open spaces of Australia there are hundreds of large active solar collectors. Passive solar energy is a simpler process designed to trap the sun's heat, and is used to heat thousands of homes. These homes have a lot of glass windows where the sun shines in to warm brick or walls and floors. The warm stonework then radiates the heat into the house at night and on cloudy days.

Animal Fact:
The adorable koala is found only in the eucalyptus forests of eastern Australia. A newborn koala weighs less than 3 ounces and spends its first 6 months in the mother's pouch.

13

Very Fancy Vegetables

*Serve these fancied vegetables to your family and friends
and "WOW" them with your gourmet cooking!*

Ginger-Glazed Carrots

Serves 4

TOOLS:
peeler
knife and cutting board
measuring cup and spoons
small saucepan with cover
strainer

INGREDIENTS:
2 cups peeled and sliced carrots
1 tablespoon honey
1 tablespoon butter
1 teaspoon ground ginger

Serving: 1/2 Cup
Protein: 1 gm
Fat: 3.5 gm

Calories: 90
Carbohydrates: 15 gm
Calcium: 30 mg

1. With adult assistance, peel and slice carrots.

2. Place carrots in saucepan with just enough water to cover them. Bring to a boil, then continue to cook, over medium-high heat for 5 minutes.

3. Strain carrots, then return to the saucepan with honey, butter and ginger. Cover and heat over low burner for 3 minutes, stirring gently.

Food Fact:
In ancient times, honey was called the nectar of the gods and was the principal sweetener used. Honey consists almost entirely of sugars, but it also contains a number of minerals, B-complex vitamins and amino acids.

Lemon Green Beans

Serves 4

TOOLS:
small skillet
measuring cups and spoons

INGREDIENTS:
3 cups steamed green beans
1 tablespoon olive oil
½ teaspoon garlic powder
3 tablespoons lemon juice
salt and pepper to taste

1. With adult assistance, heat olive oil in a skillet over medium heat.

2. Add green beans and sauté for 1 minute.

3. Add garlic powder, lemon juice and sauté another minute. Remove from heat, add salt and pepper.

Serving: 3/4 Cup	Calories: 67
Protein: 2 gm	Carbohydrates: 9 gm
Fat: 3.5 gm	Calcium: 44 mg

Earth Fact:

The natural home of a group of plants and animals is called a habitat. Try to find different habitats in your area, you shouldn't have much trouble locating one, even in your own back yard! Look around trees, under rocks and in the garden. Is there a pond nearby? Ponds are home to a large community of different plants and animals. For a fun habitat experiment, gather four chopsticks or four 10-inch long sticks, 5-feet of string or twine, a ruler, and a hammer or rock. Now find a spot that is out of the way from where you usually walk. Measure an area that is 1-foot by 1-foot square, and hammer a stick about 4-inches into the ground on each of the four corners. Wrap the string around the 4 corner "posts" and tie it in a knot. This is your observation area. Take a close look, use a magnifying glass if you have one. Over the next few days write down everything you see in the observation area, and make a map of where you found it. How many different plants, animals, and insects belong to this particular habitat? How can you protect them in their natural habitat?

15

Hodge Podge Soup

Hodge Podge Soup is made from a hodge podge of ingredients, and changes each time you make it!

Serves 6

TOOLS:
large saucepan and cover
wooden spoon
measuring cups and spoons

BASIC INGREDIENTS:
4 cups vegetable, chicken
   or beef broth
2 cups 2%-lowfat milk
1 cup left over mashed
   potatoes or prepared
   instant mashed potatoes
2 tablespoons dehydrated
   chopped onion or
   ¼ cup chopped onion
1 teaspoon marjoram
½ teaspoon garlic powder
½ teaspoon pepper

Serving: 1.5 Cups   Calories: 140
Protein: 14 gm   Carbohydrates: 16 gm
Fat: 3.5 gm   Calcium: 140 mg

YOU CHOOSE:
1 cup cooked and diced meat,
   chicken, turkey, or fish
2 cups of any combination of
the following vegetables. They
should be precooked and cut:
   asparagus
   broccoli
   beans
   carrots
   corn
   green beans
   peas
   potatoes
   rice
   summer squash
   peeled tomatoes
*Use any leftovers in the fridge
   you think would be good.*

1. Combine broth, milk and mashed potatoes in a large saucepan. Place on the stove over medium heat. Cook, stirring constantly, until blended.

2. Add onion, spices, vegetables and any other ingredients you selected. Bring to a boil. Reduce heat to low, cover and simmer 20 - 30 minutes.

Experiment using different seasonings until you find the perfect blend. Remember to only add a little bit at a time; spices should compliment, not overwhelm, your soup. Try oregano, thyme, basil, parsley, paprika... Check out your spice cupboard and ask the adults in your house what their favorite combinations are.

Animal Fact:
Animals that share the same habitat often rely on each other for survival. A balance exists between such species, and survivial is dependent on the amount of food available. Wolves were once a common sight in the United States and Europe until people cut down large areas of forest to build homes, upsetting the balance of nature and the habitat of the wolves' prey. When their food source dwindled or dissappeared, wolves began preying on farm animals for their survival, and were shot by farmers. Reforestation and preservation programs are now allowing wolves to return to places where they once roamed wild.

Food Fact:
Using mashed potatoes is a great way to enrich creamed soups and stews without the fat and calories of cream. Cook potatoes in your soup until they are tender, scoop some out, mash, then stir back in.

17

Chicken Salad Platter

Serves 4

TOOLS:
knife and cutting board
measuring cups and spoons
medium mixing bowl and spoon

INGREDIENTS:
½ cup chopped cucumber
½ cup chopped celery
½ cup chopped sweet red
    pepper
2 cups cooked diced chicken
½ cup plain yogurt
½ cup mayonnaise
¼ teaspoon garlic powder
¼ teaspoon ground ginger
¼ teaspoon dill weed
⅛ teaspoon pepper
3 cups chopped spinach
1 cup alfalfa sprouts
2 sliced peaches,
    fresh or canned

Serving: 1/4 Recipe   Calories: 282
Protein: 25 gm   Carbohydrates: 13 gm
Fat: 14.5 gm   Calcium: 102 mg

1. With adult assistance, chop cucumber, celery and red pepper.

2. In mixing bowl, combine cucumber, celery, red pepper, chicken, yogurt, mayonnaise and spices. Blend well.

3. With adult assistance, chop spinach. Place ¾-cup of chopped spinach on each of 4 serving plates.

4. Sprinkle alfalfa sprouts over spinach. Spoon chicken mixture on top and surround with sliced peaches.

Animal Fact:
Sea otters are found along the shores of the North Pacific. They sleep and eat floating on their backs. One of their favorite foods is fresh clams, which they crack with a rock to get at the meat inside. These adorable creatures were once hunted for their fine, silky brown fur, but are now protected by international law.

Food Fact:

Growing sprouts is fast and easy! They are ready to eat in just 3-5 days.

1) Buy untreated alfalfa, radish or dill seeds.

2) Measure 1-tablespoon of seeds into a quart jar. Cover seeds with warm water and let them sit overnight.

3) The next day, pour off the water. Cover the top of the jar with a piece of cheesecloth and secure in place with a rubber band around the rim.

4) Put the jar of seeds under the sink or in a dark cupboard. For best results, lay the jar on its side.

5) Rinse the sprouts twice a day through the cheesecloth. Pour off all the water each time.

6) After 3 - 5 days, rinse sprouts thoroughly and drain. Sprouts will stay fresh in an airtight container in the refrigerator for about a week.

Tuna Treats

TOOLS:
non-stick spray cooking oil
muffin tin
can opener
small mixing bowl
measuring cups
fork

INGREDIENTS:
6 oz. white tuna,
　　packed in water
1 slice dry bread
1 egg
1 egg white
½ cup cooked peas
¼ cup grated cheddar cheese

Serving: 2 Patties	Calories: 333
Protein: 38 gm	Carbohydrates: 13 gm
Fat: 13 gm	Calcium: 241 mg

Preheat oven to 350°. Spray 4 muffin tin cups with non-stick cooking oil.

1. Open tuna can. Leaving the lid in place, gently press lid into can draining excess liquid into the sink. Use a fork to flake tuna from can into a mixing bowl.

2. Crumble dry bread over tuna, then add egg, egg white and peas. Stir with a fork until blended.

3. Press about one-quarter of the mixture into each of 4 muffin cups. Sprinkle tops with grated cheddar. Fill unused muffin cups half full with water and bake 15 minutes.

Serve on a bed of lettuce with carrot sticks on the side for a healthy lunch.

Food Fact:
Look carefully at the tuna can to be sure that it has the "dolphin safe" emblem on it. Tuna with this emblem is caught using "long lines" instead of nets that can also trap and drown dolphins.

Ecology Fact:
Coral reefs are beautifully formed shapes of various colors, sizes and textures, made from the skeletal remains of millions of tiny corals. A coral is a type of invertebrate. An invertebrate is an animal without a backbone that supports its body with a tiny shell. When these small organisms die their shell remains, and other living corals grow upon it. Over time, a coral reef habitat is created that feeds and shelters many higher forms of life, including more than 1,500 species of saltwater fish. One of the biggest threats to coral reefs is the growing population in tourist areas where reefs grow. Increasing human populations in these areas create larger quantities of sewage which are discharged into the shallow seas. Nutrients from the sewage encourage algae growth on the reef, which eventually cover over and kill the coral. Coral reefs also suffer when careless divers trample on them, boat anchors drag over and rip apart reefs, or when they are chipped at for souvenirs.

Rice & Bean Casserole

TOOLS:
knife and cutting board
skillet
measuring cups and spoons
can opener
2-quart covered casserole dish

INGREDIENTS:
1 medium onion
2 teaspoons canola oil
1½ cups water
1 tablespoon vegetable or
    beef bouillon granules
1 cup uncooked long grain rice
½ teaspoon dried marjoram
15-oz. can chopped stewed
    tomatoes
15-oz. can kidney beans
1 cup canned white beans
½ cup grated cheddar cheese

Serving: 1/4 Recipe   Calories: 412
Protein: 20 gm   Carbohydrates: 66 gm
Fat: 8 gm   Calcium: 223 mg

Preheat oven to 350°.

1. With adult assistance, peel and chop onion.

2. Heat canola oil in skillet. Sauté onion in oil for 2 minutes. Add water and bouillon granules, bring to a boil.

3. Stir in rice, marjoram, stewed tomatoes and beans.

4. Pour into 2-quart casserole dish. Cover and bake 50 - 60 minutes, or until liquid is absorbed.

5. Remove from oven and sprinkle with grated cheese.

*Serve with fresh hot cornbread
for a hearty meal!*

Animal Fact:
Parrots inhabit most tropical and southern temperate regions of the world. Most are fruit and seed eaters, and some also eat insects. Their large hooked bills are strong enough to chisel open the toughest of nuts, and are used like a third foot when climbing. These colorful birds usually live for 30 - 50 years.

Ecology Fact:
Rain forests are home to at least three-fourths of the earth's wildlife. Millions of plant and animal species live there, and new species are discovered there everyday. The rain forests play a vital role in regulating the world's climate through the oxygen, carbon and water cycles. Many medicines are made from plants that grow only in the rain forest, and scientists are sure many more cures will be found from the species that live there. In the communities next to the rain forests, increasing human population and impoverished conditions cause people to cut the rain forest trees for building materials and to create farmland. Rich nations also demand these timbers for furniture, paper and construction projects. Almost half of the world's rain forests have already been destroyed, and the cutting continues. You can help by recycling newspapers, cardboard and product packaging, and not wasting paper. Please remember to never buy furniture made from rain forest trees, such as teak and mahogany.

23

Zesty Chicken & Broccoli Bake

Serves 6

TOOLS:
saucepan
measuring spoons and cups
knife and cutting board
skillet
2-quart casserole dish

INGREDIENTS:
1½ cups chicken broth
1½ chicken breast fillets
1 small green pepper
2 celery stalks
1 small onion
1 tablespoon canola oil
2 cups broccoli florets
2 teaspoons garlic powder
¼ teaspoon each paprika,
    fines herbes and pepper
1½ tablespoons cornstarch
¼ cup cold water
1 cup grated cheddar cheese

Serving: 1/6 Recipe Calories: 206
Protein: 21 gm   Carbohydrates: 8 gm
Fat: 10 gm   Calcium: 173 mg

1. In a saucepan, bring chicken broth to a boil. Add chicken, cover and poach 20 minutes, or until the inside of the chicken meat is white.

2. Remove chicken, but leave the poaching liquid in the saucepan.

3. With adult assistance, dice chicken, green pepper, celery and onion into small pieces.

4. Heat canola oil in skillet over medium heat. Add chicken, diced vegetables and broccoli florets. Sauté 4 minutes, then remove skillet from heat.

5. Stir seasonings into the vegetables. Heat left in the pan will help to release their flavors. Preheat oven to 350°.

6. Return the saucepan with poaching liquid to the stove, and bring to a boil. In a small cup, dissolve cornstarch in cold water, then mix it into the boiling liquid, lower heat and simmer until thickened.

7. Pour the thickened broth over chicken and vegetables in the casserole dish. Stir in grated cheese. Bake 20 minutes or until bubbly.

Ecology Fact:

Energy is vital for many of our basic needs, such as cooking, heating and transportation. Some methods used for producing energy can seriously damage our environment. Safer and cleaner forms of energy production are now being introduced in many countries. These are renewable energy sources, meaning they will not run out as will the earth's supply of fossil fuels. Renewable energy sources include solar energy, wind, wave and tidal energy, and the burning of industrial waste and consumer refuse. These resources are used to create electricity with far less risk to the environment. There are things your family can do to make a difference:

1) Don't waste electricity. Turn off lights when not in use. Take a shower instead of a bath, it uses less heated water.

2) Insulate hot water tanks and pipes. The water will heat up quicker and stay hot longer.

3) Insulate your attic and draft proof doors and windows. This can save up to 20% of your energy bill (leaving more money for fun things)!

Creamy Ziti and Rice

Serves 4

TOOLS:
2 covered cooking pots
wooden spoon
strainer
8" x 8" baking dish
measuring cups and spoons
blender

INGREDIENTS:
2 cups ziti pasta
1 cup brown rice
1 cup spaghetti sauce
½ cup plain yogurt
¼ cup cottage cheese
¼ teaspoon onion powder
¼ teaspoon garlic powder
⅛ teaspoon salt
⅛ teaspoon pepper
1 cup grated mozzarella
    cheese

Serving: 1/4 Recipe   Calories: 548
Protein: 21 gm   Carbohydrates: 89 gm
Fat: 12 gm   Calcium: 283 mg

Preheat oven to 350°.

1. Boil ziti and rice in separate pots, following the package directions. Drain, then combine in baking dish.

2. Combine ¼-cup of spaghetti sauce with yogurt, cottage cheese, onion powder, garlic powder, salt and pepper in blender. Blend until smooth. Stir in ½-cup of the grated cheese.

3. Spoon mixture over pasta and rice, stir gently to coat. Cover with remaining ¾-cup of spaghetti sauce, and ½-cup of grated cheese. Bake 15 minutes or until bubbly.

Food Fact:
Folklore expounds the benefits of yogurt as a cure for insomnia, a wrinkle remover, and even as the fountain of youth. Although these claims may be exaggerated, yogurt is a very valuable food. One cup provides over 50% of the daily calcium requirement. A healthy form of bacteria obtained from yogurt lives in our intestines and produces the essential B vitamins.

Earth Fact:
About 40% of the world's land mass is mountainous. A considerable amount of rain and snowfall accumulates in the mountains. These majestic regions gradually release water from melted snows and overflowing mountain lakes into rivers and streams. This supplies us with the water we use in our homes and businesses, and is also used to create energy. The Himalayas are a mountain system in Asia, on the northern edge of India. They are the highest mountain range in the world and include Mount Everest. Topping 29,108 feet above sea level, Mount Everest is the highest mountain in the world. In the lower elevations of the Himalayas, destruction of the rain forest contributes to global warming, the loss of habitat for wildlife and soil erosion. Major reforestation programs are now under way. In a number of years the trees planted by volunteers will form a strong network of roots, holding the soil in place and supporting many other forms of life in the rain forest.

Animal Crackers

Serves 8

TOOLS:
measuring cups and spoons
blender
sifter
mixing bowl
pastry cutter
small saucepan
rolling pin
cookie cutters
non-stick cookie sheet

INGREDIENTS:
1 cup dry oatmeal
¼ teaspoon salt
½ cup white flour
¼ teaspoon baking soda
¼ cup butter
2 tablepoons honey
¼ cup buttermilk
1 teaspoon vanilla

Serving: 1/8 Recipe   Calories: 141
Protein: 3 gm   Carbohydrates: 18 gm
Fat: 7 gm   Calcium: 11 mg

Preheat oven to 350°.

1. With adult assistance, set up blender and grind ½-cup of oatmeal until it becomes a fine oat flour.

2. Sift together oat flour, salt, white flour and baking soda. *

3. Use pastry cutter to cut butter into flour mixture until crumbly. Stir in remaining ½-cup of oatmeal.

4. Heat honey and buttermilk together over low heat until honey dissolves. Remove from heat, add vanilla, and stir into flour mixture.

5. On a lightly floured surface, roll out cracker dough until about ¼-inch thick. Cut with animal shaped cookie cutters, then place on a non-stick cookie sheet. Bake 10-12 minutes.

* CHOCOLATE ANIMAL CRACKERS:
Add 1½-teaspoons unsweetened cocoa powder to dry ingredients, and increase the amount of honey in step 4 to 4-tablespoons.

Earth Fact:
The oceans of the world form one vast ecosystem covering over 70% of the planet's surface. Besides supporting a wide variety of different species, the oceans supply humankind with a steady flow of nutritious food, water, energy and minerals. The underwater landscape is just as varied as the above water landscape, with countless different habitats and communities. There are underwater expanses of barren sand flats, huge mountain ranges and areas rich in plant and animal life. Almost all of the ocean's plant and animal life exist within 325 feet of the surface where sunlight can penetrate. For far too long, people thought that getting rid of waste at sea was safe and it would be quickly diluted. However, toxins build up in the water and affect the health of sea animals. Help preserve our oceans by never leaving litter on the beach. You can also get involved with local organizations which work to stop companies from dumping their waste into rivers and streams, because it eventually ends up in our magnificent oceans.

Chocolate Chip Oatmeal Cookies

Makes 3 Dozen Cookies

TOOLS:

2 large mixing bowls
measuring cups and spoons
electric or hand mixer
large spoon and a spatula
cookie sheet
non-stick spray cooking oil

INGREDIENTS:

½ cup butter
1½ cups packed brown sugar
2 eggs
½ cup applesauce
2 teaspoons vanilla
1½ cups all-purpose flour
1 teaspoon baking soda
¼ teaspoon salt
½ teaspoon cinnamon
3 cups oats
1 cup flaked coconut
1 cup chocolate chips

Serving: 2 Cookies	Calories: 309
Protein: 5 gm	Carbohydrates: 46 gm
Fat: 12 gm	Calcium: 56 mg

Preheat oven to 350°.

1. In a large mixing bowl, beat together butter and brown sugar until light and fluffy. Add eggs, applesauce and vanilla, and beat until smooth.

2. In a separate bowl, combine flour, baking soda, salt and cinnamon. Fluff with a fork to mix. Add to butter and brown sugar mixture in the large bowl. Beat until smooth and creamy.

3. Stir in oats, coconut and chocolate chips.

4. Spray cookie sheet with non-stick cooking oil. Drop 12 rounded teaspoons of dough onto cookie sheet (3 cookies across and 4 down). Bake 10 minutes, or until light brown.

5. Remove sheet from the oven but leave cookies on the sheet to cool 2 - 3 minutes. Use the spatula to remove cookies and place them on wire rack. Repeat steps 4 and 5 for remaining cookie dough.

Store cookies in an airtight container.

Recycling Fun:
The three "R's" of recycling are: reduce, reuse and recycle. Reusing items instead of throwing them away can be fun as well as functional. Here are some tips for reusing common waste items.

1) Cereal boxes look great on a bookshelf storing magazines or school papers. Cut off the top at an angle, then wrap the cereal box in newspaper "funnies".

2) Birds will flock to your homemade birdfeeder made from washed out cardboard milk cartons or plastic soda bottles. (Be sure to include a perch.)

3) Chase away the rainy day blues and turn garbage into giggles. Use colorful cut-outs from product packaging and scraps of aluminum foil for collages, homemade cards and game pieces. Make bowling pins from plastic soda bottles. Egg cartons make great paint palettes and flat plastic lids are safe indoor frisbees. Just be sure everything you use is clean and dry.

4) Make an observation notebook using the back side of used paper. Punch holes and thread ribbon or twine through them to bind your notebook. Then decorate the front with pressed leaves and flowers.

Applesauce Celebration Cake

Stirring up a celebration is easy when it is mixed and baked all in the same pan!

Serves 9

TOOLS:

8" x 8" square cake pan
measuring cups and spoons
fork
small mixing bowl
non-stick spray cooking oil

INGREDIENTS:

1¼ cups all-purpose flour

½ cup whole wheat flour

½ cup sugar

½ teaspoon salt

1 teaspoon baking soda

2 teaspoons cinnamon

¼ teaspoon nutmeg

1 teaspoon vanilla

1 tablespoon vinegar

3 tablespoons canola oil

1 cup unsweetened applesauce

Serving: 1 Piece   Calories: 184
Protein: 3 gm   Carbohydrates: 33 gm
Fat: 5 gm   Calcium: 13 mg

Preheat oven to 350°.

1. Spray cake pan with non-stick cooking oil.

2. Measure the dry ingredients into the cake pan, and blend together thoroughly with a fork. Make 3 holes in the blended dry ingredients.

3. Put the vanilla into the first hole, the vinegar into the second, and the canola oil into the third.

4. Spoon applesauce into cake pan, and use a fork to blend everything together. Bake 35 - 40 minutes.

After cake has completely cooled, frost and decorate as desired. To serve, cut into 9 pieces.

Food Fact:

Use applesauce in baked goods to replace part or all of the oil. This lowers the fat and calorie content while retaining moisture.

Cream Cheese Frosting

Makes 1½ Cups

TOOLS:
measuring cups and spoons
small mixing bowl
fork

INGREDIENTS:
1 cup lowfat cream cheese
1½ cups powdered sugar
1 teaspoon vanilla
3 tablespoons 2%-lowfat milk

Serving: 2 Tablespoons   Calories: 109
Protein: 5 gm   Carbohydrates: 21 gm
Fat: 0.5 gm   Calcium: 29 mg

Soften cream cheese by taking it out of the refrigerator 1 hour before making the frosting.

1. In a small mixing bowl, mash cream cheese with powdered sugar.

2. Add vanilla and milk, blend well.

Ecology Fact:
Many well-known plants and animals are endangered. Here are some things you can do to protect animals where you live:
1) Don't collect butterflies, wildflowers, or any other living thing. Study creatures only in their natural habitat.
2) Keep your dog on a leash if there are animals or nesting birds around.
3) Never buy objects made from ivory, coral, sponges or shells.
4) Respect all living things. Even spiders, moths and ants are useful and necessary for ecological balance.

33

Peach Cobbler

Serves 9

TOOLS:
medium saucepan
wooden spoon
measuring cups and spoons
8" x 8" non-stick cake pan

INGREDIENTS:
⅓ cup sugar
1 tablespoon cornstarch
½ teaspoon cinnamon
¼ teaspoon nutmeg
4 cups sliced peaches,
      fresh or canned
1 teaspoon lemon juice
Drop Biscuits dough, page 35

Serving: 1 Piece   Calories: 242
Protein: 5 gm   Carbohydrates: 42 gm
Fat: 6.5 gm   Calcium: 92 mg

Preheat oven to 350°.

1. If using canned peaches, drain.

2. Mix sugar, cornstarch, cinnamon and nutmeg in the saucepan. Stir in peaches and lemon juice. Cook over medium heat, stirring constantly, until mixture boils for 3 minutes.

3. Pour peaches into cake pan. Top with spoonfuls of biscuit dough. Bake 25 - 30 minutes. Cool in pan before cutting into 9 servings.

Food Fact:
Peaches are believed to have originated in China. In spite of the peach tree's short life, its fruit was a symbol of immortality to the ancient Chinese. They exchanged peaches as tokens of affection, and placed bowls of peaches in the tombs of loved ones.

Drop Biscuits

Makes 12 Biscuits

TOOLS:
sifter and fork
measuring cups and spoons
non-stick cookie sheet

INGREDIENTS:
2 cups flour
2 tablespoons sugar
1 tablespoon baking powder
¼ teaspoon salt
¼ cup butter
¾ cup buttermilk
1 egg

Serving: 1 Bisuit   Calories: 132
Protein: 3 gm   Carbohydrates: 19 gm
Fat: 5 gm   Calcium: 64 mg

Preheat oven to 350°.

1. Sift together flour, sugar, baking powder and salt.

2. Cut butter into flour mixture by mashing with a fork until crumbly.

3. Whisk together buttermilk and egg, then stir into flour mixture, just until dough forms a ball.

4. Place spoonfuls of dough on the non-stick cookie sheet, leaving space between them. Bake 15 minutes.

For baked dough topping: Drop dough by the spoonful over Peach Cobbler, pot pie or stew. Bake as directed.

Ecology Fact:
Acid rain is created from gases released by factories and road vehicles, and by the burning of coal and oil for fuel. These gases react with sunlight and air moisture to produce rain that has a high ph level, also known as "acidic". The effects of acid rain can be devastating to many forms of life. It changes the levels of chemical components in soil, causing trees to lose their leaves and die. The corrosive rain can even eat away at the features of statues. Most affected by acid rain are lakes, rivers and streams which become too acidic for aquatic life to live. Where the problem is most severe, lime is dumped into the water body to neutralize the acid. Help reduce acid rain by conserving energy: turn off lights, minimize the use of heating and air conditioning, and walk, bike or carpool when possible.

Chocolate Pudding

Serves 4

TOOLS:
measuring cups and spoons
medium saucepan
whisk
4 dessert cups

INGREDIENTS:
2 cups 2%-lowfat milk

⅓ cup sugar

¼ cup cornstarch

¼ teaspoon salt

3 tablespoons unsweetened
   cocoa powder

1 teaspoon vanilla

½ tablespoon butter

4 tablespoons whipped topping

1. Combine milk, sugar, cornstarch, salt and cocoa powder into a medium saucepan. Whisk until blended.

2. Whisking constantly, bring the mixture to a boil over medium heat. Pudding burns if you stop stirring.

3. Reduce the heat to low. Boil gently 2 - 3 minutes (keep stirring). Remove from heat.

4. Add vanilla and butter. Let pudding cool in saucepan for 15 minutes, stirring once or twice. Spoon ½-cup pudding into each of 4 dessert cups. Top each cup with a tablespoon of whipped topping. YUM!

Serving: 1 Dessert Cup   Calories: 193
Protein: 5 gm   Carbohydrates: 34 gm
Fat: 4 gm   Calcium: 169 mg

Food Fact:
Chocolate is made from the seeds, or "beans", of the tropical cacao tree. The beans are inside leathery pods that grow on both the trunk and branches of the tree. Workers cut the pods from the tree with large knives called machetes. The purple or creamy white beans are shelled from the pod. At this stage, the bean has a raw bitter taste. It is a long process before it becomes the sweet creamy treat we know as chocolate.

Ecology Fact:

The two largest ecological concerns are waste and the depletion of our natural resources. Every year, Americans throw away 50 billion food and drink cans, 27 billion glass bottles and jars, and 65 million plastic and metal jar and can covers! Over 80% of this garbage is sent to landfills. One big way that each of us can make a difference is by recycling. These are some simple things you can start doing to help:

1) Return all deposit soda bottles and cans to store or recycling center.
2) Separate glass, paper and other recyclable materials and take them to a recycling center. (see page 7)
3) Pack your lunch in reusable containers.
4) Bring a cloth bag to the store to carry your purchases home.
5) Use silverware and dishes instead of disposables at home and on picnics.
6) Use paper grocery bags for garbage instead of purchased plastic bags.
7) Get information from your local library on how to start a compost pile. Composting provides rich nutrients for gardening and greatly reduces waste.
8) Speaking of gardens, plant one! Produce from a garden is healthier, and reduces the amount of processed foods and manufactured packaging.

Frozen Fruit Fizzle

Serves 1

TOOLS:
measuring cups and spoons
blender
tall glass

INGREDIENTS:
2 tablespoons frozen apple
    juice concentrate
1 cup frozen mixed fruit
6 ice cubes
½ cup sparkling water

Serving: 1 Recipe   Calories: 137
Protein: 1 gm   Carbohydrates: 35 gm
Fat: 0.5 gm   Calcium: 23 mg

1. With adult assistance, combine apple juice concentrate, fruit and half of the ice in a blender. Blend at medium speed until smooth. (If your blender has a pulse button, use this at the beginning to get things going.)

2. Add remaining ice cubes. Blend at high speed for 45 seconds or until smooth. Pour into a tall glass, add sparkling water and stir. Slurp with a straw.

Earth Fact:
An ice sheet covers nearly all of Antarctica. At its thickest point the ice sheet is almost 3 miles deep! The Antarctic ice was formed from the layers of snow that fell over millions of years, and never completely melted. The weight of new snow squeezes the old snow underneath until it turns into a substance called firn, which eventually becomes ice.

Orange Cream Dream

Serves 1

TOOLS:
measuring spoons
blender
tall glass

INGREDIENTS:
2 tablespoons frozen orange
    juice concentrate

½ banana
2 scoops lowfat vanilla ice cream
¼ teaspoon vanilla
3 ice cubes

Serving: 1 Recipe   Calories: 245
Protein: 4 gm   Carbohydrates: 43 gm
Fat: 7.5 gm   Calcium: 101 mg

1. Wih adult assistance, combine orange juice concentrate, banana, frozen yogurt and vanilla in a blender. Blend at medium speed until smooth, about 30 seconds.

2. Add ice cubes and blend at high speed for 45 seconds, or until smooth. (If your blender has a pulse button, use this at the beginning to get things going.) Pour into a tall glass and serve with a straw.

Animal Fact:

Seen from a distance, a colony of penguins might easily be mistaken for a group of little men. These flat-footed sea birds stand erect, and often line up in long regular files like soldiers. They walk so stately and dignified that the sight is very comical. Penguins feed under water on fish, squid and crustaceans. In fact, penguins do not know how to eat on land and only learn this skill when living in captivity at zoos and aquariums. Most penguins build their nest on the ground from pebbles, mud and vegetation. The female lays one or two chalky white eggs in the nest. The baby birds are born covered with down and need care for a long time. Half-grown penguins are often looked after in groups called creches or kindergartens. In addition to Antarctica, penguins live on subantarctic islands and on the cool coasts of Africa, New Zealand, Australia and South America.

Grape Monkey Jelly

Makes Three 2-Cup Containers

TOOLS:
measuring cups and spoons
medium mixing bowl
small saucepan
whisk
3 2-cup freezer containers

INGREDIENTS:
4 cups grape juice
5 cups sugar
1 box powdered fruit pectin

Serving: 2 Tablespoons	Calories: 197
Protein: 0 gm	Carbohydrates: 50 gm
Fat: 0 gm	Calcium: 4 mg

1. Rinse plastic containers and lids with boiling water to sterilize.

2. Measure 3-cups of grape juice into mixing bowl. Whisk in sugar.

3. In a saucepan, combine remaining grape juice with powdered fruit pectin. Bring to a boil over high heat. Stirring constantly, boil for 1 minute.

4. Pour boiled mixture into grape juice and sugar. Stir for 3 minutes to dissolve sugar.

5. Fill containers to ⅛-inch from the top. Cover and let stand at room temperature for 24 hours.

Store jelly in the refrigerator for 3 weeks or up to 1 year in the freezer.

Animal Fact:
The mountain gorilla is found mostly in the high rainforests of Rwanda and Burundi in Africa. They live in family groups lead by a single mature male. Although the combination of habitat loss and hunting has greatly reduced the gorilla population, international laws and gorilla sanctuaries in Africa now help to ensure the survival of these incredible animals.